Charles R. Swindoll

RECOVERING A PIONEER SPIRIT

ESTHER
A MODEL OF PIONEER
INDEPENDENCE

Third in a series of five mini-books, based on the lives of biblical characters who modeled an attitude of fortitude that needs to be recovered.

INSIGHT FOR LIVING

Unless otherwise identified, all Scripture references are from the New American Standard Bible, © The Lockman Foundation 1960, 1962, 1963, 1968, 1971, 1972, 1973, 1975, 1977. Used by permission.

ESTHER: A MODEL OF PIONEER
        INDEPENDENCE
© 1992 Charles R. Swindoll. All rights reserved. Published by Insight for Living, Post Office Box 69000, Anaheim, California 92817-0900.

NOTICE

Unless otherwise noted, no portion of this publication may be translated into any language or reproduced in any form, except for brief quotations in reviews, without prior written permission of the publisher.

Printed in the United States of America.

Book designed by Jerry Ford
Cover illustration by Diana Vasquez

*Committed to Excellence in Communicating
Biblical Truth and Its Application*

INTRODUCTION

The early pioneers were an independent lot. Not wanting to be hemmed in by crowded streets and houses built close to each other, they struck out for new frontiers. They chose freedom over the comforts of security.

This required their being innovative, self-reliant, and free from the need for others to help them survive through all kinds of hardship. To soft city-dwellers, rugged pioneers must have seemed fiercely inhospitable. But so life was on the frontier; everyone took care of his own gear, raised his own crops, solved his own problems, reared his own children. And, for sure, spoke his own mind.

Much of this independence of spirit has eroded in the latter half of the twentieth century. Not only are most people seldom alone, thinking through the issues of life in solitude, they rarely declare their convictions or come to their own conclusions apart from others' advice. While a measure of that is understandable and can prove helpful, the down side is an *over*-dependence on one another. The result of such extreme mutual dependence can lead to "group think," where it is believed that no one

ESTHER: A MODEL OF PIONEER INDEPENDENCE

should stand alone or hold to a position that isn't the consensus of the majority. This is worse than unfortunate; it is dangerous.

My hope is that you will find encouragement to be yourself in the pages that follow . . . and not just to be yourself, but to think for yourself—to realize the importance of cultivating your own convictions and standing up for what is right, regardless.

Several years ago I decided to teach one of the least-known books of the Bible, the book of Esther. It wasn't long before I realized that this Old Testament woman was one of the finest models of pioneer independence in all of Scripture. Because she stood absolutely alone and because she was willing to die, if necessary, for her beliefs, her people were saved from extermination. Her story must be told!

But my major and ultimate reason for writing about Esther is not that we might extol this ancient Bible character, it's that we might emulate her example. God is still interested in using each one of us; therefore, we need to become convinced of the importance of the role each of us is to play in this drama called life.

As Edward Everett Hale once wrote:

I am only one,
But still I am one.
I cannot do everything,
But still I can do something;
And because I cannot do everything
I will not refuse to do the something
  that I can do.[1]

May these pages stir up a healthy independence in all of us, so that we will begin modeling it today rather than merely admiring it in the pioneers of yesteryear.

Chuck
Chuck Swindoll
Fullerton, California

ESTHER
A MODEL OF PIONEER
INDEPENDENCE

ESTHER: A MODEL OF PIONEER INDEPENDENCE

In an overpopulated world, it is easy to underestimate the significance of *one*. With so many people who are so capable, so gifted, so intelligent, and so involved in so many important activities, *who am I?*

Simplistic though the answer may seem, you are *you* . . . the only *you* in this vast world . . . the only one with *your* face, *your* mix of gifts and voice and personality and style and sphere of influence. Just as you were born independently, so you will independently answer to God for the way you live your life. If you have borne children, you are the only birth mother your children will ever have. If you are the only Christian where you work, you—alone—are the one being watched. You are the only gospel being read.

THE SIGNIFICANT IMPACT OF ONLY ONE

In the world of art, who can measure the significance of a Da Vinci, a Michelangelo, a Disney? In the history of the military, who can measure the significance of a Lee, a Grant, a MacArthur, an Eisenhower, or a Schwarzkopf? In music, who can ever determine the impact of a Bach, a Mozart . . . Brahms, Beethoven, or Mendelssohn? Why, such individuals changed the entire course of the world!

I could go on into the subject of significant men of God who spoke for God during great eras of church history. Who could ever gauge the importance of clergymen like Augustine, Aquinas, Wycliffe, Wesley, Watts, Luther, Calvin, Whitefield, Edwards, Bunyan, Spurgeon, Moody, and Graham (to name only a few)? In fact, one could trace our way through the Scriptures just by naming individual people, very human men and women, whose lives shaped their times. God's Book is not a book about mass movement and vast crusades, but rather one story after another of one person after another, upon whose life God's hand rested. He deliberately singled out certain individuals. He still does.

Read these verses slowly. See if they don't convince you of the value of *one*.

"For the eyes of the Lord move to and fro throughout the earth that He may strongly support those whose heart is completely His. You have acted foolishly in this. Indeed, from now on you will surely have wars." (2 Chron. 16:9)

Now the Lord saw,
And it was displeasing in His sight that
    there was no justice.

And He saw that there was no man,
And was astonished that there was no
   one to intercede;
Then His own arm brought salvation
   to Him;
And His righteousness upheld Him.
(Isa. 59:15b–16)

"Roam to and fro through the streets
   of Jerusalem,
And look now, and take note.
And seek in her open squares,
If you can find a man,
If there is one who does justice, who
   seeks truth,
Then I will pardon her." (Jer. 5:1)

They forgot God their Savior,

*Who had done great things in Egypt,
Wonders in the land of Ham,
And awesome things by the Red Sea.
Therefore He said that He would
    destroy them,
Had not Moses His chosen one stood
    in the breach before Him,
To turn away His wrath from destroy-
    ing them.* (Ps. 106:21–23)

"And I searched for a man among them who should build up the wall and stand in the gap before Me for the land, that I should not destroy it; but I found no one." (Ezek. 22:30)

ESTHER: A MODEL OF PIONEER INDEPENDENCE

THE INDEPENDENT INTERCESSION OF ONE WOMAN

Just like you, little did a young Jewish girl dream she would ever become all that significant in God's scheme of things. Her name, originally, was Hadassah. She was, according to the sacred record, "beautiful of form and face." And since both her parents had died early in her life, her cousin Mordecai was rearing her as if she were his own daughter. It was in the security of that Jewish home, she learned of God's love . . . and she was trained to walk with Him. Though they lived in Persia, theirs was a godly family who feared and worshiped Jehovah.

Much to everyone's surprise, through a remarkable chain of events too lengthy to go into, Mordecai's adopted daughter found herself among the finalists in a beauty contest sponsored by the king of Persia, Ahasuerus. Whoever won was to be pronounced queen . . . Esther did and she was! What seemed so strange at the time to Mordecai and Queen Esther would later make perfect sense as God's plan for her unfolded.

Mourning and Weeping

All was not well in Persia. Through

ESTHER: A MODEL OF PIONEER INDEPENDENCE

King Ahasuerus' blind allegiance to a wicked official named Haman (whom the king had promoted to prime minister of Persia), a plot was underway to remove all the Jews from the kingdom. This plan, borne in the anti-Semitic mind of Haman, was signed into law by the king . . . which resulted in an overwhelming spirit of depression among the Jews in every province of Persia. Here is a quick glance at the scriptural record:

Haman sought to destroy all the Jews, the people of Mordecai, who were throughout the whole kingdom of Ahasuerus.

Then Haman said to King Ahasuerus, "There is a certain people scattered and dispersed among the peoples in all the provinces of your kingdom; their laws are different from those of all other people, and they do not observe the king's laws, so it is not in the king's interest to let them remain. If it is pleasing to the king, let it be decreed that they be destroyed, and I will pay ten thousand talents of silver into the hands of those who carry on the king's business, to put into the king's treasuries." Then the king took his signet ring from his hand and gave it to Haman, the son of Hammedatha the Agagite, the enemy of the Jews. And the king said to Haman, "The silver is yours, and the people also, to do with them as you please." Then the king's scribes were summoned on the thirteenth day of the first month, and it was written just as Haman commanded to the king's satraps, to the governors who were over each province, and to the princes of each people, each province according to its script, each people according to its language, being written in the name of King Ahasuerus and sealed with the king's signet ring. And letters were sent by couriers to all the king's provinces to destroy, to kill, and to annihilate all the Jews, both young and old, women and children, in one day, the thirteenth day of the twelfth month, which is the month Adar, and to seize their posses-

sions as plunder. A copy of the edict to be issued as law in every province was published to all the peoples so that they should be ready for this day. The couriers went out impelled by the king's command while the decree was issued in Susa the capital; and while the king and Haman sat down to drink, the city of Susa was in confusion.
(Esther 3:6b, 8–15)

What a sight! Removed from the anguish among the Jews in Persia, the king and Haman sat quietly in the palace totally indifferent to the wholesale confusion that swept through every Jewish heart.

ESTHER: A MODEL OF PIONEER INDEPENDENCE

- What can possibly be done?
- Who could ever change the decree?
- How might anyone help—Jew or Gentile?

After all, this was one of those infamous "laws of the Medes and the Persians" which no one could change. But, always remember, what is impossible among men is possible with God. The Jews may have been paralyzed by grief, but God remained in full control. No matter how powerful earthly authorities may be, God still rules!

Esther, like the king, was unaware of all the confusion and grief the edict had caused. In fact, she knew nothing of the decree . . . so Mordecai took it upon himself to inform her of the holocaust that would soon transpire.

When Mordecai learned all that had been done, he tore his clothes, put on sackcloth and ashes, and went out into the midst of the city and wailed loudly and bitterly. And he went as far as the king's gate, for no one was to enter the king's gate clothed in sackcloth. And in each and every province where the command and decree of the king came, there was great mourning among the Jews, with fasting, weeping, and wailing; and many lay on sackcloth and ashes.

ESTHER: A MODEL OF PIONEER INDEPENDENCE

Then Esther's maidens and her eunuchs came and told her, and the queen writhed in great anguish. And she sent garments to clothe Mordecai that he might remove his sackcloth from him, but he did not accept them. (4:1–4)

Mordecai was conducting a one-man protest. He hated what was being planned by Haman and the only thing he knew to do was appeal to Queen Esther. Finally, they made contact.

Informing and Responding.

Then Esther summoned Hathach from the king's eunuchs, whom the king had appointed to attend her, and ordered him to go to Mordecai to learn what this was and why it was. So Hathach went out to Mordecai to the city square in front of the king's gate. And Mordecai told him all that had happened to him, and the exact amount of money that Haman had promised to pay to the king's treasuries for the destruction of the Jews. He also gave him a copy of the text of the edict which had been issued in Susa for their destruction, that he might show Esther and inform her, and to order her to go in to the king to implore his favor and to plead with him for her people.

And Hathach came back and related Mordecai's words to Esther. (vv. 5–9)

ESTHER: A MODEL OF PIONEER INDEPENDENCE

For the first time, the queen was made aware of the edict . . . the plan for the extermination of her people. Her stomach must have churned when she read of the plan "to destroy, to kill, and to annihilate all the Jews, both young and old, women and children, in one day"!

People in authority cannot respond appropriately without the facts. So Mordecai was determined to equip his adopted daughter, the queen, with the facts. The rest was up to her. Her first response was less than Mordecai had anticipated.

Then Esther spoke to Hathach and ordered him to reply to Mordecai: "All the king's servants and the people of the king's provinces know that for any man or woman who comes to the king to the inner court who is not summoned, he has but one law, that he be put to death, unless the king holds out to him the golden scepter so that he may live. And I have not been summoned to come to the king for these thirty days." And they related Esther's words to Mordecai. (vv. 10–12)

To some measure we can understand Esther's initial response. The rules of the court were well-known and strongly enforced. Not even the queen could burst into the inner court without being invited. For her

ESTHER: A MODEL OF PIONEER INDEPENDENCE

to do so apart from his summons could mean her death. In this case, however, Mordecai urged her to ignore protocol and risk that possibility. After all, the lives of thousands—in fact, tens of thousands—hung in the balance.

His "speech" may have been brief, but it is one of the finest in all the Old Testament. Appealing to her conscience, Mordecai presses the issue and pleads that she stand alone and do the hard thing.

Pleading and Praying.

Then Mordecai told them to reply to Esther, "Do not imagine that you

*in the king's palace can escape any
more than all the Jews. For if you remain silent at this time, relief and de-
liverance will arise for the Jews from
another place and you and your father's
house will perish. And who knows
whether you have not attained royalty
for such a time as this?" Then Esther
told them to reply to Mordecai, "Go,
assemble all the Jews who are found
in Susa, and fast for me; do not eat
or drink for three days, night or day.
I and my maidens also will fast in the
same way. And thus I will go in to the
king, which is not according to the law;
and if I perish, I perish." So Mordecai
went away and did just as Esther had
commanded him.* (vv. 13–17)

ESTHER: A MODEL OF PIONEER INDEPENDENCE

The key statement in Mordecai's message to Esther is that penetrating question: "And who knows whether you have not attained royalty for such a time as this?" Clearly, it must have been that question that stirred Esther into action.

Her options were not that many. Here was Mordecai's logic:

- If she did nothing, not even she would escape the extermination. After all, she was also Jewish!

- The Jews will ultimately survive. God isn't limited to this game plan. His promise for their survival was greater than her involvement . . . but how great it would be if she were the one God intended to use to fulfill His plan.

- Who knows? This might be the very reason she had been given the title as queen. If so . . . everything would make sense!

Esther, though still a young woman, demonstrates remarkable character at this point. She reveals a "pioneer spirit" of independence as she decides (against all odds) to break protocol and step into the king's presence, uninvited, and plead for the survival of her people. How admirable are her words! "If I perish, I perish." Suddenly, in one short sentence, Esther shows a depth of

ESTHER: A MODEL OF PIONEER INDEPENDENCE

character rarely found among those in positions of authority. She is willing to put her life on the line for the sake of a principle.

I appreciate one man's appraisal of this pioneer of independence:

The moment Haman surfaced, Esther began to move from being a beauty queen to becoming a Jewish saint, from being an empty-headed sex symbol to being a passionate intercessor, from the busy-indolent life in the harem to the high-risk venture of speaking for and identifying with God's people.[2]

Have you noticed how the entire scene has shifted?

- From fear to abandonment
- From hesitation to determination
- From concern for her own safety to the preservation of the people

What wonderful changes! And they emerged because Esther—only one among so many—decided to act independently, courageously.

The result? You need to read the balance of the book of Esther to get the whole picture . . . but the bottom line is this: God honored her decision. She went before the king, she represented the cause of right, and the edict was overturned. In fact, Haman was hanged on the gallows he had built for Mordecai.

What a surprise ending! But when God is in control, surprises aren't all that uncommon. In the end, He always wins! What makes this particular story so unique is that it underscores once again the impact one person can make in a situation that seems so bleak—in fact, virtually impossible to change.

THE INDEPENDENT INVOLVEMENT OF ONE PERSON—YOU!

Returning to my opening line, in an overpopulated world, it is easy to underestimate the significance of *one*. That is especially true when that "one" happens to be *you*.

As Mordecai appealed to Esther, I want to close these pages by appealing to you today. There are critical issues in our day that require involvement—personal and independent involvement—if we hope to stand for the cause of right. To list only a few:

- standing against abortion
- sheltering the homeless
- providing for the hungry and destitute
- assisting those struggling with addictions
- helping the abused, the neglected
- working with the developmentally disabled

- curbing the crime rate
- protecting children
- solving the out-of-control pornography problem
- getting involved in school/educational issues
- voting for those who represent a standard of righteousness

A couple of concluding principles come to mind. First, not until we believe one person can make a difference will we be willing to risk.

Read that sentence again, please. I believe it with all my heart. It has been true in my own life, and I have noticed it is true in the lives of those with whom I have worked. Becoming a model of "pioneer independence" starts with this very real risk... but what a sense of satisfaction it can bring! It is, in fact, a sacred duty.

All this reminds me of a few lines which represent a prayer from one of the grand hymns of the church:

Set our feet on lofty places,
Gird our lives that they may be
Armored with all Christlike graces
In the fight to set men free.
Grant us wisdom, grant us courage,
That we fail not man nor Thee,
That we fail not man nor Thee.[3]

In some cases in life, you—you, alone—must stand up, speak out, and set forth your convictions. To do less than that is to fail both your fellow human beings and your Lord.

Second, only when we move from the safe harbor of theory to the rugged path of reality do we actually *make* a difference.

It is relatively easy to find others who are willing to debate, discuss, and dialogue about life's crucial issues. Talk is cheap; therefore, those who prefer talk to involvement are many. But it is not until we leave that popular place of safety and actually get on the pioneer trail of reality (as Esther decided to do) that our convictions will make any difference.

May I be painfully honest with you? There are some who read these pages who are still much too dependent on others. While I certainly am aware of the value of others' support and the importance of cultivating a circle of friends, I have observed that this can develop into an overdependence, where the presence of others becomes *essential* to one's happiness and security. That is both an unhealthy and an unbiblical extreme. Those who grow toward maturity in their walk with the Lord finally learn the importance of no longer "needing" others in order to survive. If you happen to be in that category, you may find

ESTHER: A MODEL OF PIONEER INDEPENDENCE

the following words as helpful as I did when I first read them. The anonymous piece is entitled:

After Awhile

After awhile
you learn the subtle difference
between holding a hand
and chaining a soul

and you learn
that love doesn't mean leaning
and company doesn't mean
security

and you begin to learn
that kisses aren't contracts
and presents aren't promises

RECOVERING A PIONEER SPIRIT

and you begin
to accept your defeats with your
head up and your eyes open
with the grace of an adult
not the grief of a child

and you learn
to build your roads on today
because tomorrow's ground
is too uncertain for plans

After awhile
you learn that even sunshine burns
if you get too much
so plant your own garden
and decorate your own soil
instead of waiting for someone
to bring you flowers

ESTHER: A MODEL OF PIONEER INDEPENDENCE

*and you learn
that you really can endure
that you really are strong
and you really do have worth*[4]

My hope is that God would free all of us from needing the approval of others in order to feel fulfilled. In addition, I pray that these few pages about the life of one woman who saved a nation will motivate us to be less afraid to think and then act independently.

When all other models fade from our memory, may the person of Christ remain firm and clearly visible. I know of no better example of the right kind of independence than

He who, alone, bore our sins on that rugged cross.

ESTHER: A MODEL OF PIONEER INDEPENDENCE

Dear Lord,

The time-worn words of Isaac Watts seem so relevant as we wrap up our thoughts on this subject:

Am I a soldier of the cross?
A foll'wer of the Lamb?
And shall I fear to own His cause
Or blush to speak His name?

Are there no foes for me to face?
Must I not stem the flood?
Is this vile world a friend to grace,
To help me on to God?

Sure I must fight if I would reign—
Increase my courage, Lord!
I'll bear the toil, endure the pain,
Supported by Thy Word.[5]

Ours is a hostile environment, Lord. It seems to be against anything that is morally just and committed to integrity. This world is no friend that helps us walk with You. On the contrary, it places obstacles in the path that leads to You and the accomplishment of Your will.

While we realize that You are not dependent on any one of us to accomplish Your plan, it is clear from Your Word that You desire to use those whose heart is truly committed to You. But it is equally clear that that calls for an independence rarely found in the rank and file of humanity.

In light of these things, Heavenly Father, raise up a few strong-hearted soldiers of the cross who are willing to stand in the gap, regardless of the risks. Make us people of principle, straight-thinking followers of the Lamb, who neither blush to speak Your name nor hesitate to represent Your cause.

We need help in knowing how to be independent without being obnoxious . . . in discerning what is worth fighting for and what should simply be ignored . . . in remaining accountable and responsible to others without becoming so in need of others that we lean on them instead of You.

Give us a heart like ancient Esther. Remind us of the importance of fulfilling our individual role, no matter the sacrifice or cost. And when we have done so, may we remember the One who gets the glory.

> *In the name of Jesus
> our model and our master,
> Amen.*

NOTES

1. *Bartlett's Familiar Quotations*, 15th ed., rev. and enl., ed. Emily Morison Beck (Boston, Mass.: Little, Brown and Co., 1980), p. 590.

2. Eugene H. Peterson, *Five Smooth Stones for Pastoral Work* (Atlanta, Ga.: John Knox Press, 1980), p. 173.

3. Harry Emerson Fosdick, "God of Grace and God of Glory," in *The Hymnal for Worship and Celebration* (Waco, Tex.: Word Music, 1986), no. 292.

4. An Ogden Hall Resident, "After Awhile."

5. Issac Watts, "Am I a Soldier of the Cross?," in *The Hymnal for Worship and Celebration*, no. 482.